# Parris

GW00992139

Alexandra Carr-Malcolm

## Introduction

Parris is Alexandra's third anthology. It is based on the themes of love, longing, loss, and death.

The poems take inspiration from Irish mythology and also from the legendary poet, song writer, and musician - Philip Parris Lynott.

## Acknowledgements

Thanks to the editor, Kate Garret, from Three Drops from a Cauldron for publishing Liath Macha.

Photo credit, front cover – Ha'penny Bridge Dublin by coolriff - courtesy of www.iStockphoto.com

**Legal Notice:**

## Dedication

For Patrick, Oliver, and Kiran.

Also for the extended Thin Lizzy Family who keep the legacy of Phil's music alive.

# Index

## Dublin

I never went to Dublin,

or strolled along the shore.

I never walked on Grafton Street,

or wore the pearls you swore.

I never came to visit you,

and relive bygone days;

to welcome ghosts that haunted me,

or weep upon your grave.

## Liath Macha

Here is where the silence lies,

wishing on the lashes of a dead man's eyes.

There is where death doeth break,

memories and dreams are left in its wake

A love like ours will never ever die,

carried by the winds through a midnight sky.

Kiss the stars and brush the moon,

cherish each heartbeat as they pass too soon.

Waning moons and riptide seas,

facing our mortality whilst on our knees.

Breath stops short, the world goes on,

the meaning of our life has all but gone.

A world without you can never ever be,

an organic shift in humanity.

Broken hearts rang through the skies,

the universe broke down the day you died.

## Parris

What should you do when all hope is gone,

and the memory pain lingers on and on?

When the tablets you take, take all your words,

and the pills that cure ills, consume all your
verbs.

You reach for the bottle, that's what you do,

the one that says drink me, to change your
world view.

Eat the cake that says 'Eat Me', and don't leave
a crumb,

then repeat the refrain until you feel numb.

Don't look through the glass, you won't like
what you see,

and old aged reflection that I call me.

## Black Rose

The last of the summer rays

blush gently on my cheek.

Tears fall like dew from the morning rose.


The flower blossoms,

the flower blooms.

Slowly it fades

as petals fall

one by one

the spirit

is gone.

I wear my heart upon my sleeve,

I also wear my rose.

Both are there for you to see.


The flower blossoms,

the flower blooms.

Slowly it fades

as petals fall

one by one

the spirit

is gone.


The last rose of summer cries.

The heart beats deathly slow.

The sun has set beneath the skies.

The flower blossoms,

the flower blooms.

Slowly it fades

as petals fall

one by one

the spirit

is gone.

## Howth

Eye of Ireland

the heart of Cuchulainn's Clan

is calling me home

## We Three

We walked on the beach,
my friend, the dog, and me;
looked out to the seas,
and plotted our dreams,
my friend, the dog, and me.

We danced on the beach,
my friend, the dog, and me;
we thanked lucky stars,
couldn't believe where we are,
my friend, the dog, and me.

We strolled on the beach,
my friend, the dog, and me,
we sat in the dunes,
reflecting on tunes,
my friend, the dog, and me.

We stood on the beach,

my friend, and me;

wondering where the time had gone,

and how life had moved on,

my friend, and me.


Looking back at the beach,

just me;

the gulls mourn the song,

of where it all went wrong,

just me — and my memories.

## Lonely Romeo

Tsamhraidh days of purple haze, love hung low in the air,

Romeo and Julia sing summer blues without a care,

heartbeats, completes, repeats the sweet refrain,

the memory pain of nostalgia plays, his essence still remains.

## Night Star

When you left,

you took us all with you,

the old, the young, the Saints and the Sinners.

A gaping chasm,

left in your wake.

Three decades of grief,

the tides of loss,

your fall from grace,

as you plummeted us all,

into oblivion.

Yet – you shine brighter,

and more fierce,

than any star,

I've ever seen.

## Taking Liberties

Living in the Liberties,
they took our lives, they took our dreams,
we took their wives, and ne'er paid tax,
they took our jobs, we paid them back.

Libertines and petticoat dreams,
a lucky penny, threadbare seams,
St Stephen's Green sleep Heugenots
malversation broke their lot.

We wove the wool, pulled o'er our eyes,
the silk sipped still, tongues tasted lies,
they passed the buck, we shot them back,
they ground us down, and broke our backs.

## City Angel

When our names are marble dust

and stars adorn our souls

the fable of our foundling love

will ring the skies no more

my cries for you will still be seen

through adamantine eyes

cloaked in the shroud of ever-night

sagacious shooting stars

## King's Call

We did not have the internet,

no mobile phones to intercept,

the tragic news that wounded souls,

our hearts became the blackest holes.


All the King's horses

and all the King's men

could not put our hearts

back together again


We gathered at the Wapentake,

the DJ played your songs till late,

not a single soul knew what to do,

so we just drank a toast to you.


All the King's horses

and all the King's men

could not put our hearts

back together again

The disbelief stretched on for years,

our love for you, honoured by our tears,

The King calls out a sweet refrain,

in music, solace, soothes the pain.

## Hiraeth

He has the eye of Ireland,

and the old Fand soul,

Liffey tears course his veins.

The Auld Town whispers his name,

the seas are calling him home.

Over beaches and o'er borders,

carried home by White Horses,

to the shores, to be sure of Hiraeth.

## Freedom to Fly

Let go, let go, and let go some more,

pluck up your courage, and give up the floor,

lift up your feet, one at a time,

spread your wings, and lift up your eyes.

Take flight to the skies, where the inky stars
live,

feel the air rush, and learn to breathe.

Let go of this life, and let yourself go,

soar up to freedom, give up what you know,

What can you see from your bird's eye view?

Does it all feel strange, is it shiny and new?

Fly far away, where the old souls reside,

play with the moon, from the worldlings do
hide,

and in the morning when you awake,

cherish your dreams in the life that you make.

## The Bloody Stream

when the music is done

and the lights have gone down

the last train has gone

and you sit all alone

with a heart-stone for comfort

the flowers have faded

and all tears have fallen

there is nothing left

but the blue skies

and bird song

## Borders

The startling cry of something wakes me

the syrupy darkness sugars my mind

in my dreams my mother is guiding me

through all the underworlds of sleep

my heart tells me I'm in Derry

my head tells me I'm in Dublin

as my eyes focus through the sentimentality

I see I am at home

and outside, the cat calls

in forlorn search for love

**1982**

You placed a cassette tape on the speaker,
with two concert tickets for The City Hall on
8pm - Monday 26th April 1982

I was swotting for exams at the time,
and the tape remained abandoned until
8pm - Sunday 25th April 1982

Felling obliged, I slid the tape into the deck,
and listened again, and again, till morning
8am – Monday 26th April 1982

My first live concert, my first love, twin guitars,
repeat the refrain, I fell in love
8pm – Monday 26th April 1982

Thirty five years on, my resolve never faded,
tape turned to vinyl, and now you're both gone
8pm - Wednesday 26th April 2017

## Rock Star

as

the

lights went

down, and the curtain

came up, charisma and long legs filled the night

mirrored Fender catches light

and, Oh, those Irish eyes

daring                    you to

fall                         deep

go                                         on

## About the Author

### Alexandra Carr-Malcolm

Alexandra Carr-Malcolm was born and raised in Chesterfield, Derbyshire. She now lives in Yorkshire and works as a freelance British Sign Language Interpreter.

Alex has been featured in collaborative anthologies by Dagda Publishing, Three Drops Press, and The Wait. She has also been featured in several themed series, hosted by Silver Birch Press, and other online sites such as, Three Drops from a Cauldron, The Blue Hour, and Yellow Chair Review.

### Other Books by the Author

Tipping Sheep (the right way)
Lulu (2013)

Counting Magpies
Beswick and Beswick (2015)

**Connect with Alexandra Carr-Malcolm**

http://www.worldlywinds.com

https://www.facebook.com/AlexandraCarr-Malcolm

https://twitter.com/Alexcm_poet

76100229R00020

Made in the USA
Columbia, SC
29 August 2017